Why do tigers have stripes?

Disney BOOKS BY MAIL

When Mickey Wonders Why, he searches out
the answers with a little
help from these friendly experts:

Vice President and Publisher Cathryn Clark Girard
Director, Product Development Kristina Jorgensen
Editorial Director Lisa Ann Marsoli

DK Direct Limited
Managing Art Editor Eljay Crompton
Senior Editor Rosemary McCormick
Writer Alexandra Parsons
Illustrators The Alvin White Studios and Richard Manning
Designers Amanda Barlow, Veneta Bullen, Richard Clemson,
Sarah Goodwin, Diane Klein, Sonia Whillock

Contents

Why are polar bears white?

So that when they go out hunting it's hard to see them moving across the snow and ice. Polar bears live at the cold, icy north pole. Their thick, white, furry coats help them blend into their snowy home.

Look – no nose!
You would think their shiny black noses would give them away, but polar bears aren't dumb. They cover their noses with snow. But what's Mickey going to do about those ears?

Ice say, ice say!
What do polar bears
eat for lunch?
Icebergers

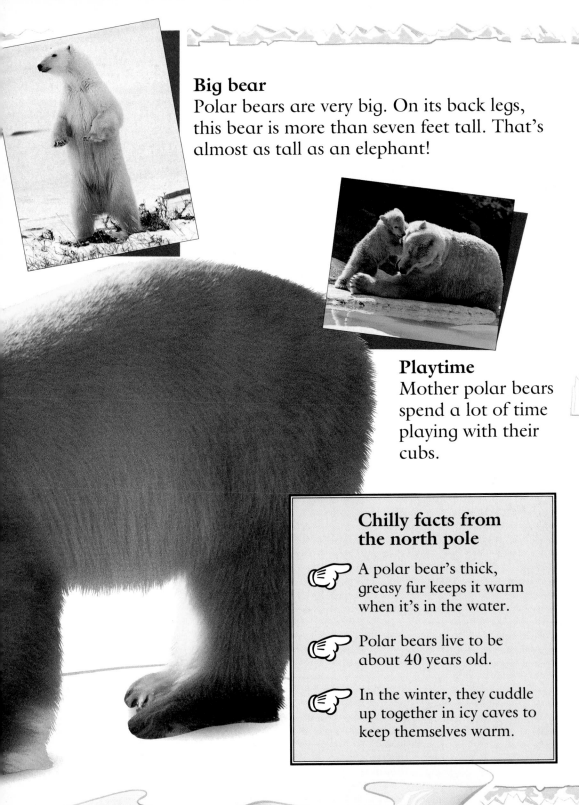

Big bear
Polar bears are very big. On its back legs, this bear is more than seven feet tall. That's almost as tall as an elephant!

Playtime
Mother polar bears spend a lot of time playing with their cubs.

Chilly facts from the north pole

 A polar bear's thick, greasy fur keeps it warm when it's in the water.

Polar bears live to be about 40 years old.

In the winter, they cuddle up together in icy caves to keep themselves warm.

Why does a stick insect look like a stick?

So hungry birds, bats, and lizards will leave it alone. After all, would you want to eat a stick for dinner? But just looking thin and twiggy isn't enough. The stick insect has learned to hold its body in a stick-like way and to KEEP VERY STILL!

6

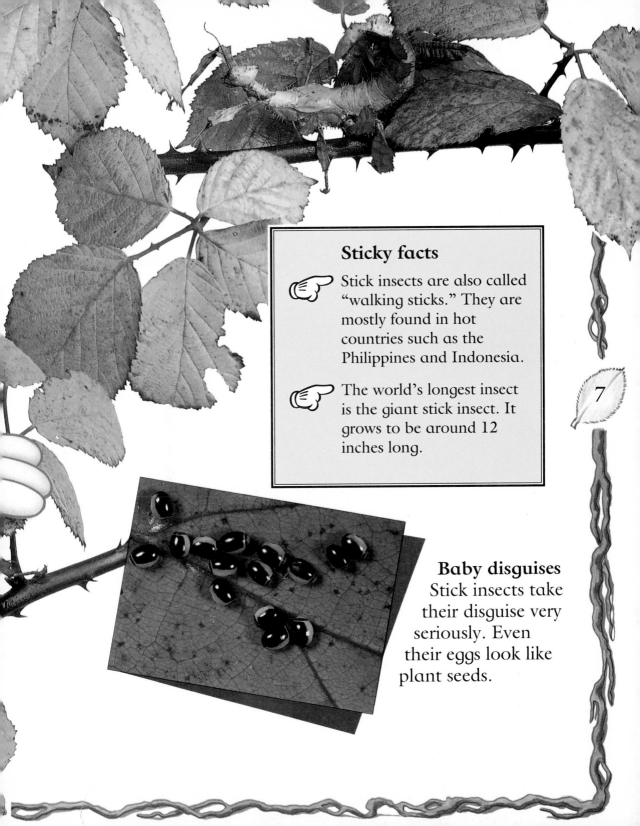

Sticky facts

☞ Stick insects are also called "walking sticks." They are mostly found in hot countries such as the Philippines and Indonesia.

☞ The world's longest insect is the giant stick insect. It grows to be around 12 inches long.

Baby disguises
Stick insects take their disguise very seriously. Even their eggs look like plant seeds.

Why do tigers have stripes?

So they can't be seen.
A tiger's stripes blend in
with the dark and light
colors of the plants and
grasses where it lives. Also,
the stripes break up the
outline of the tiger's body,
making it difficult for other
animals to see it.

Which way?
A tiger's stripes, on the main
part of its body, run up and
down. But Mickey's stripes are
going the wrong way. Oh no!

Tiger tales

☞ When they get hot, tigers cool off with a swim.

☞ Angry tigers wrinkle up their noses and snarl.

☞ Tiger cubs are looked after by their mother until they are about two years old. She teaches them how to hunt by playing games with them.

Human disguises

People have learned from animals how to hide without being seen. Warships were once painted with wavy lines so, from far away, the enemy couldn't see the shape of the ship clearly.

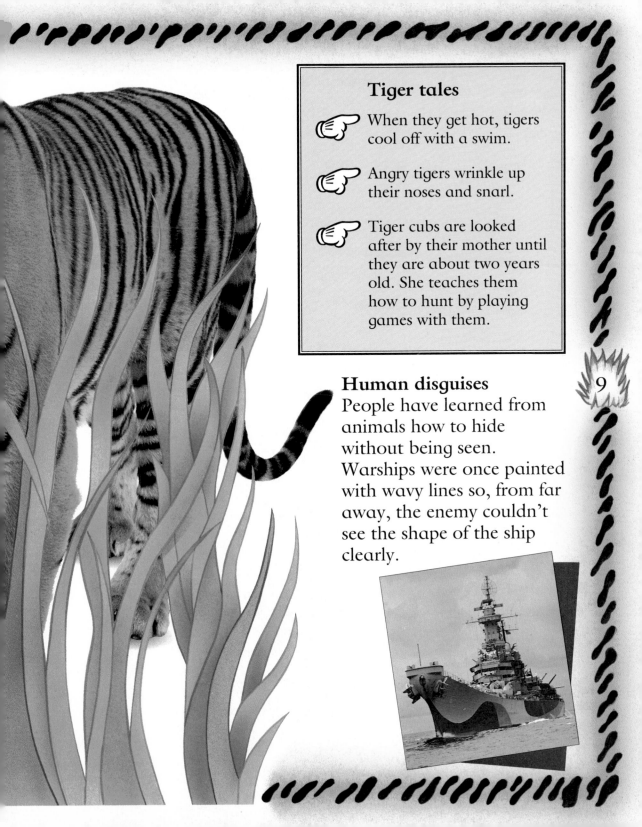

Why does a crocodile look like a log?

So it can sneak up on its lunch. "I'll just have a cool drink from this river," thinks a passing antelope. "Just a few old logs floating around in it, nothing to be frightened of." Well, we know different!

Croc surprise!
What do you get if you cross a
crocodile with a flower?
**I don't know, but I wouldn't try
smelling it!**

Crocodile tales

People used to think that crocodiles
cried when they ate their prey. Now we
know they cry to get rid of the salt they
have swallowed in the water.

Doing the tail walk
Crocs can rear up on
their powerful tails
and push themselves
through the water.

Thanks for the ride, Mom!
Crocodiles lay eggs on the
river bank. Loving crocodile
moms carry their babies to
the river in their mouths.

Why are some birds' eggs speckled?

So they don't look like eggs. The speckles make the shape of the egg hard to see among the leaves and branches of a tree or the stones and pebbles of the shore.

Fooled again!

The cuckoo doesn't make a nest of her own, she lays eggs in other birds' nests.

Little and large

The biggest egg in the world is the ostrich egg, which would make enough scrambled eggs for 24 people. The smallest egg is a hummingbird's egg. It's the size of your little fingernail.

Eggy facts

To protect its eggs, the Indian woodpecker lays them inside the nests of stinging ants. No one would touch the eggs with all those nasty ants around.

How do chameleons change color?

Good question! Chameleons have spots of different colors all over their skin. When it needs to change color, the chameleon's eyes and skin send messages to its brain. Then these spots shrink or grow to match the chameleon's background.

Lick lick!
Chameleons' tongues are as long as their bodies. Their long tongues help them to catch insects.

Colorful chameleon facts

☞ The chameleon also changes color when it's angry – it breaks out in red and orange spots!

☞ Chameleons live in hot places like Africa and parts of the United States.

☞ They like to eat insects, especially yummy spiders.

Eye eye!
Chameleons can look backward and forward at the same time because their eyes don't move together like ours do.

Why are some fish flat?

So that when they are swimming along they don't look like fish at all. That way bigger fish won't chase them. When danger is near they press their bodies flat against the ocean floor and blend in with their background.

What's that?
It isn't a flatfish, it's a monkfish. But it acts like a flatfish. It has a flat bottom, which it presses against the ocean bed.

Fish face
When flatfish are little, they look just like any other fish. Then one eye starts to move over to the other side of their body as they grow.

Magic eyes

A flatfish can also blend in with its background. Its eyes look at a color and its body changes to match that color. Flatfish can look like pebbles, sand, or seaweedy rocks.

Flatfish facts

If you put a flatfish on a checkerboard it will change to match the board.

The biggest flatfish is the halibut. It can grow up to 10 feet, from nose to tail. That's as long as a canoe!

How does a snake play hide and seek?

Snakes have patterns on their skins. The patterns match their background so well, they can hide without being seen – and wait for a tasty meal! But there are some snakes that have another way of protecting themselves. They lie still with their mouths open and pretend to be dead. Mickey was so still this snake didn't even notice him.

Time for a change
As snakes get bigger, a new layer of skin is made underneath the old one. Then, when the new skin is ready, the snake crawls right out of its old skin.

Slithering facts

Snakes don't have noses. They "taste" the air by sticking out their tongues.

The longest snake in the world is the regal python, which can grow to over 30 feet long — that's almost as long as a railroad car.

Fangs a lot!
Many snakes have fangs that curve in, so once they have bitten into their prey it can't escape.

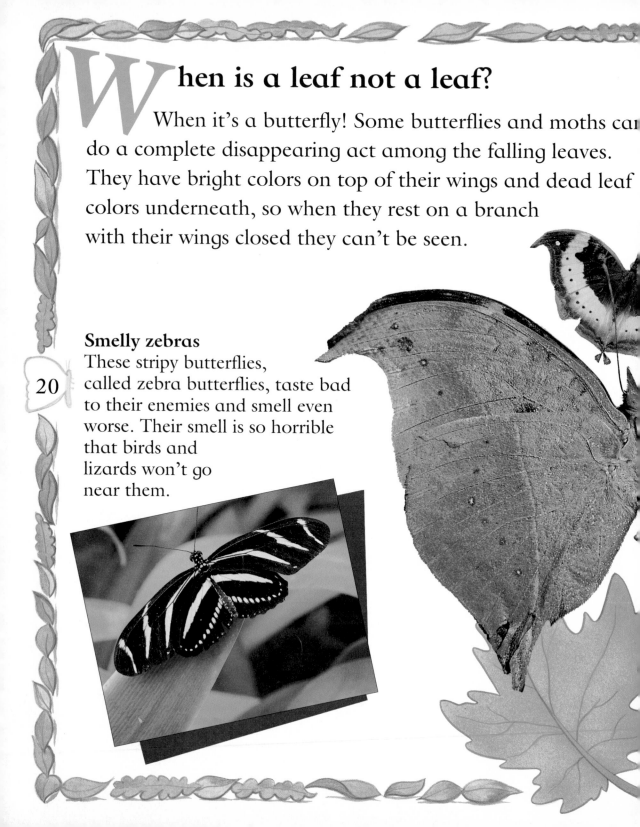

When is a leaf not a leaf?

When it's a butterfly! Some butterflies and moths can do a complete disappearing act among the falling leaves. They have bright colors on top of their wings and dead leaf colors underneath, so when they rest on a branch with their wings closed they can't be seen.

Smelly zebras
These stripy butterflies, called zebra butterflies, taste bad to their enemies and smell even worse. Their smell is so horrible that birds and lizards won't go near them.

Leaf me alone

☞ Some leaf-look-alikes even have edges on their wings that look like they've been chewed by insects.

☞ There are moths that are patterned to look like the bark of trees.

☞ The European moth keeps its enemies away by looking like a nasty wasp.

Why can a baby deer not be spotted?

Because it IS spotted! A baby deer can stand up and walk a few hours after it is born. But until it is big enough to join the herd it hides among grasses and ferns, its spotty coat making it very difficult to see.

Santa's deer
Reindeer live in the cold north. Both male and female reindeer have antlers. Male deer use their antlers to frighten off other male deer who try to take over their herd.

Oh, deer!
There are many kinds of deer. This is a male red deer. It has big, bony antlers on its head.

Deer me
What do reindeer say before they
tell a joke?
This one will sleigh you!

23

Deer facts

Grown-up male red deer
are called stags, and the
females are called hinds.

The tiniest deer is the
Chinese water deer. It's
only 20 inches tall. The
male has two sharp
tusks poking out of
its mouth.

How do caterpillars look like snakes

The hawk moth caterpillar from Brazil has markings on its body that look like snake eye So when it puffs out its chest, it looks like small, but very unfriendly snake.

Insect humor
What's a caterpillar?
**A worm with a
sweater on!**

Not just caterpillars!
Lots of insects stay alive by making their enemies think they are another, much more frightening, insect.

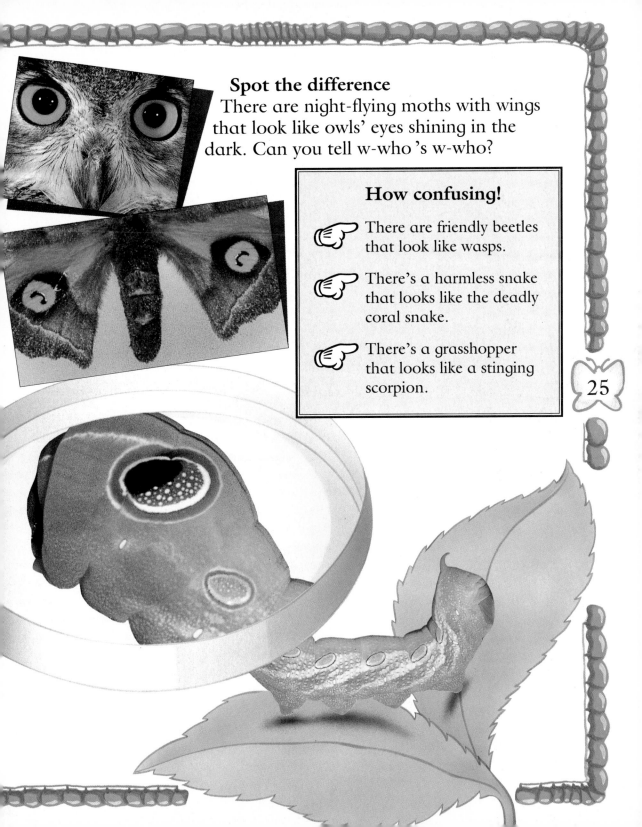

Spot the difference

There are night-flying moths with wings that look like owls' eyes shining in the dark. Can you tell w-who's w-who?

How confusing!

☞ There are friendly beetles that look like wasps.

☞ There's a harmless snake that looks like the deadly coral snake.

☞ There's a grasshopper that looks like a stinging scorpion.

25

Why are sloths so slimy?

Because they NEVER wash! After a while a sloth's fur grows a greenish scum and beetles and moths come to live in it. This may be uncomfortable, but it is a good disguise. The sloth looks just like a mossy old branch.

Hanging around
Sloths spend their days hanging upside down in trees. Their legs are strong and their claws are long and curved so they can hold on tight.

Upside-down facts

☞ Mother sloths even give birth to their babies while hanging upside down.

☞ The babies hold onto their mothers for up to nine months, until they are ready to start hanging upside down all by themselves.

27

What a drag!
Sloth legs weren't made for walking. If a sloth accidentally lands on the ground, it drags itself along with its hooked claws.

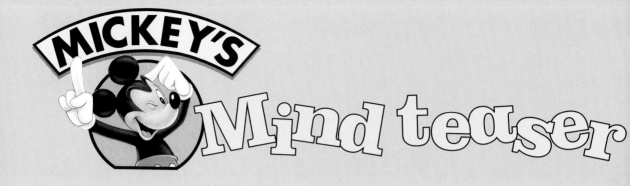

MICKEY'S Mind teaser

Many animals protect themselves by blending in with their backgrounds.

Can you find a fish, a snake, a butterfly, and some eggs in this picture?